Spotlight on Our Future

MENTAL HEALTH IN OUR WORLD

JANARI AUDRA

New York

Published in 2022 by The Rosen Publishing Group, Inc.
29 East 21st Street, New York, NY 10010

Copyright © 2022 by The Rosen Publishing Group, Inc.

All rights reserved. No part of this book may be reproduced in any form without permission in writing from the publisher, except by a reviewer.

First Edition

Editor: Theresa Emminizer
Book Design: Michael Flynn

Photo Credits: Cover FamVeld/Shutterstock.com; (series background) jessicahyde/Shutterstock.com; p. 4 Chanintorn.v/Shutterstock.com; p. 5 Lapina/Shutterstock.com; p. 7 Mita Stock Images/Shutterstock.com; pp. 8, 9 Print Collector/Hulton Archive/Getty Images; p. 10 Stock Montage/Archive Photos/Getty Images; p. 11 Encyclopedia Britannica/Universal Images Group/Getty Images; p. 12 Library of Congress/Corbis Historical/Getty Images; p. 13 Alfred Eisenstaedt/The LIFE Picture Collection/Getty Images; p. 14 kate_sept2004/E+/Getty Images; p. 15 Monkey Business Images/Shutterstock.com; p. 17 Rich Polk/Getty Images; p. 18 Florent Vergnes/AFP/Getty Images; p. 19 Sumy Sadurni/AFP/Getty Images; p. 21 Manuela Durson/Shutterstock.com; p. 22 kittirat roekburi/Shutterstock.com; p. 23 LightField Studios/Shutterstock.com; p. 25 Marla Aufmuth/Getty Images; p. 26 Neilson Barnard/Getty Images; p. 27 Shannon Finney/Getty Images; p. 29 Wavebreakmedia/iStock/Getty Images.

Library of Congress Cataloging-in-Publication Data

Names: Audra, Janari, author.
Title: Mental health in our world / Janari Audra.
Description: New York : PowerKids Press, [2022] | Series: Spotlight on our future | Includes index.
Identifiers: LCCN 2020005262 | ISBN 9781725324121 (library binding) | ISBN 9781725324091 (paperback) | ISBN 9781725324107 (6 pack)
Subjects: LCSH: Mental health--Juvenile literature. | Mental illness--Juvenile literature.
Classification: LCC RA790.53 .A93 2022 | DDC 362.196/89--dc23
LC record available at https://lccn.loc.gov/2020005262

Manufactured in the United States of America

Some of the images in this book illustrate individuals who are models. The depictions do not imply actual situations or events.

CPSIA Compliance Information: Batch #CSPK22. For further information contact Rosen Publishing, New York, New York at 1-800-237-9932.

CONTENTS

WHAT IS MENTAL HEALTH? 4

COMMON MENTAL ILLNESSES 6

MENTAL HEALTH IN THE PAST 8

A NEW ERA 12

DIFFERENCES AND SIMILARITIES 14

AT-RISK GROUPS 16

GLOBAL HEALTH 18

THE WORK OF CAREGIVERS 20

STEPPING UP 22

TECH TOOLS 24

TEEN ACTIVISTS AT WORK 26

WHAT YOU CAN DO 28

THE FUTURE OF MENTAL HEALTH 30

GLOSSARY 31

INDEX 32

PRIMARY SOURCE LIST 32

WEBSITES 32

CHAPTER ONE

WHAT IS MENTAL HEALTH?

When you think of your health, you might think of getting a cold or the flu. That's part of your physical, or bodily, health. Mental health is very important too. Mental health is about the well-being of your mind. It means having a healthy mind, healthy behaviors, and healthy ways of coping with life's pressures.

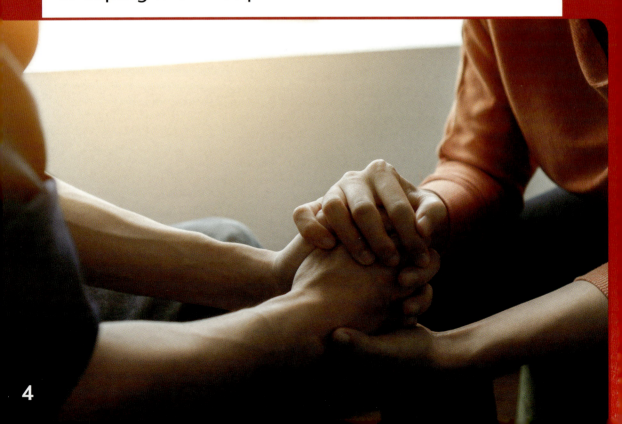

There are many different factors that affect mental health.

Many adults and children suffer from poor mental health. Mental health is important to overall health. Experts agree that there's a mental health **crisis** around the world. This affects both individuals and countries. It hurts people, and it can harm economies when people can't contribute to society.

Activists of all ages are already helping solve this problem. You can do your part to help too! Learning about mental health and understanding what it means is important for all people.

CHAPTER TWO

COMMON MENTAL ILLNESSES

Health groups say that one in four people will deal with a mental or brain disorder in their lifetime. In the United States, about 17 percent of people ages 6 to 17 deal with mental health problems.

These numbers may be even higher than what's reported. Many people don't seek help for their mental health issues. There's often a social **stigma** surrounding mental illness. Health **advocates** are working to help this problem.

Anxiety **disorders** are some of the most common mental health issues. Depression is another big problem. This is an illness in which a person deals with feelings of sadness or hopelessness for a long period of time.

Suicide, or killing oneself, is also connected to mental health issues. Almost 1 million people die each year by suicide.

Anxiety and depression are often linked.

CHAPTER THREE

MENTAL HEALTH IN THE PAST

People with mental illness have often been treated poorly. Many people didn't understand mental issues. In earlier centuries, many people believed that mental illness was rooted in the supernatural, or things that can't be explained by science. The methods used to "help" patients often harmed them or even killed them.

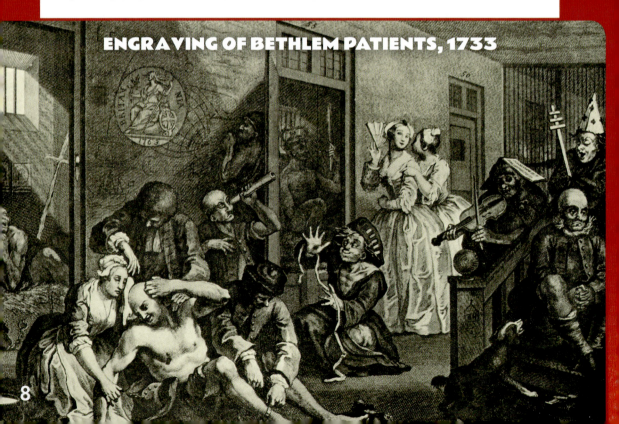

ENGRAVING OF BETHLEM PATIENTS, 1733

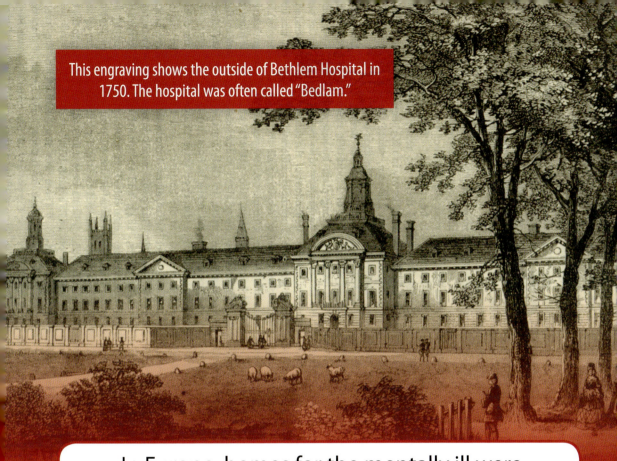

This engraving shows the outside of Bethlem Hospital in 1750. The hospital was often called "Bedlam."

   In Europe, homes for the mentally ill were often more like prisons than hospitals. Patients were treated as if they had no feelings at all. At Bethlem Royal Hospital in London, England, workers often tied up and mistreated patients. In the 1600s and 1700s, people could pay to watch the patients like they were animals in a zoo.
   Not all societies treated the mentally ill so badly, however. Some early Hindu and African **cultures** treated the mentally ill with more understanding than Europeans did.

Slowly, views about the mentally ill began to change. In the late 1700s, a French doctor named Philippe Pinel made the first attempts at real **therapy**. He removed the chains from some of his patients. Some of them had been tied up for 30 to 40 years.

An English businessman named William Tuke also pushed for better treatment. He started a retreat that used humane, or kind, treatment. In the United States, Benjamin Rush fought for better treatment for patients too. Rush was a doctor and a signer of the Declaration of Independence.

BENJAMIN RUSH

Dorothea Dix spent 40 years working for humane hospitals for the mentally ill. She died in 1887.

Dorothea Dix was one of the most famous advocates for the rights of those with mental issues. Dix began working for reform in the 1800s. She wanted more hospitals to treat the mentally ill with kindness and understanding.

CHAPTER FOUR
A NEW ERA

As time went on, views on mental health continued to change. In 1908, Clifford Whittingham Beers published a book that told of his treatment in mental hospitals. This raised awareness about many problems. This was the start of the modern mental health movement.

After World War II, many soldiers returned home with mental health issues due to their wartime experiences. In 1946, the U.S. Congress passed the National Mental Health Act. This led to the creation of the National Institute of Mental Health (NIMH) in 1949. The organization still exists today.

Clifford Beers' book *A Mind That Found Itself* raised awareness about mental health issues.

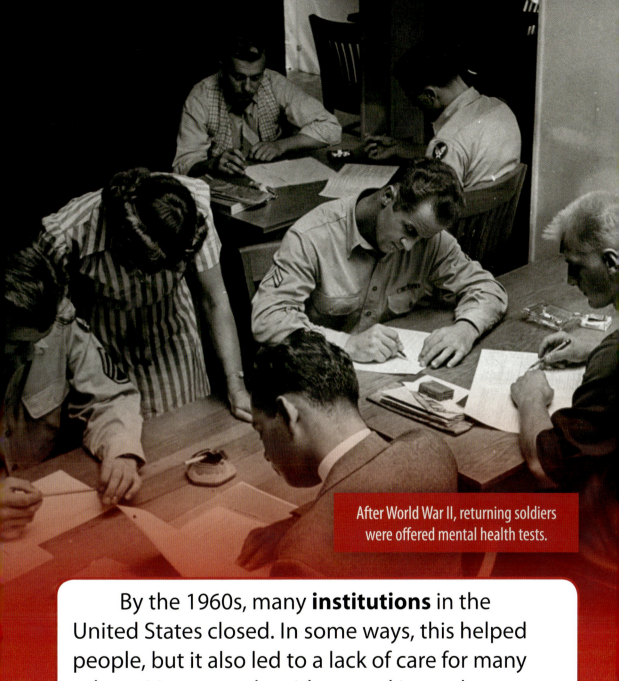

After World War II, returning soldiers were offered mental health tests.

By the 1960s, many **institutions** in the United States closed. In some ways, this helped people, but it also led to a lack of care for many others. Many people with mental issues became homeless. Others wound up in prison. This problem continues today.

CHAPTER FIVE

DIFFERENCES AND SIMILARITIES

People of all ages and races can experience mental health problems. Black and Hispanic Americans have lower reported rates of depression than white Americans, but it's more likely to last. People who identify as being two or more races are most likely to report mental illness. American Indians and Alaska Natives are more likely to suffer from alcohol issues. They also have a greater instance of post-**traumatic** stress disorder, or PTSD. This is a mental disorder that can result from a traumatic event such as war or **abuse**. White Americans die by suicide more than any other ethnic group.

People from **minority** groups are less likely to seek care for mental health issues.

　　There can be many reasons for these differences. Language issues or lack of health insurance may keep people from getting help. Other people might not get help because of the stigma of mental illness.

CHAPTER SIX
AT-RISK GROUPS

The term "LGBTQ" stands for "lesbian, gay, bisexual, transgender, queer or questioning." LGBTQ people are at special risk of mental illness. They may deal with bullying and mistreatment by family. Without family support, they may not be able to get help and treatment. They may worry that looking for help will out them to their friends and family, even if they're not ready.

Ose Arheghan is a teenage activist from Ohio who focuses on LGBTQ issues. Arheghan uses the pronoun "they." While in high school, Arheghan noticed how often LGBTQ issues and mental health issues overlapped. They decided to get involved with the Trevor Project, a national nonprofit that helps young LGBTQ people. Arheghan continues to work for change as a student at Ohio State University.

Activist Ose Arheghan was named Student Advocate of the Year at the 2017 GLSEN Respect Awards in California.

CHAPTER SEVEN

GLOBAL HEALTH

There's a shortage of mental health professionals around the globe. In fact, they make up only 1 percent of all health-care workers. Nearly half the world lives in a country with less than one psychiatrist, or a doctor who treats mental health disorders, per 100,000 people.

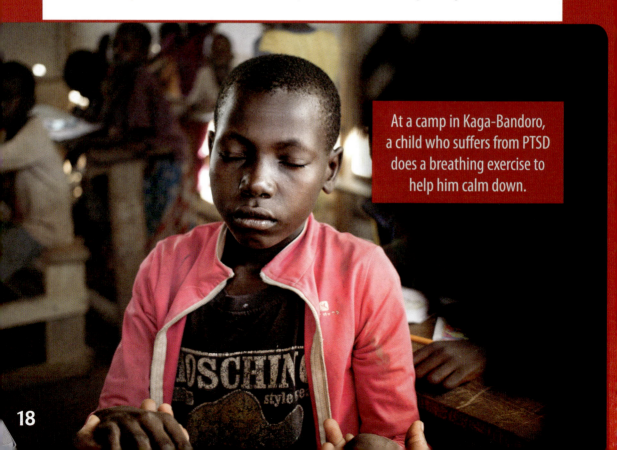

At a camp in Kaga-Bandoro, a child who suffers from PTSD does a breathing exercise to help him calm down.

People in war-torn countries often have difficulty getting the health care they need.

The good news is that activists are working to help. In 2018, Pavel Reppo created a program called mindfullwe, which is now called Finemind. Finemind's goal is to help people in need get better mental health care, even when psychiatrists aren't easily available. Reppo's experiences with obsessive-compulsive disorder, or OCD, moved him to create the program. It focuses on using communities to give people the tools they need to cope with mental health issues. Community members can help support one another even when professional health-care workers aren't available.

CHAPTER EIGHT
THE WORK OF CAREGIVERS

Mental health issues affect everyone. In the United States alone, more than 8 million Americans are caregivers to people with mental or emotional illnesses. Caring for loved ones who are suffering from mental illness can take its toll on a family. Family members and people who care for those dealing with mental illness need support.

Suicides can affect a whole community. Since 2001, the overall rate of suicide in the United States has increased by 31 percent. Many family, friends, and community members can be affected by suicide, including those who never even knew the person who died. This can include emergency teams and workers who help family members after a suicide. A 2016 study reported that a single suicide affects 115 people.

Suicide affects many people, even those who didn't know the person who died.

CHAPTER NINE

STEPPING UP

There are more effects from mental health issues. About 20 percent of homeless people and 40 percent of prisoners in the United States suffer from a serious mental health issue. In addition, 70 percent of young people in the **juvenile** court system have a mental health problem.

It's important for all people to have access to the mental health services they need.

A national organization called the Stepping Up Initiative helps deal with some of these problems. The Stepping Up Initiative works to keep people with mental illness out of jails by getting them the help they need. It also connects people in jail with mental health services. The Stepping Up Initiative trains people how to spot mental illness so that they can help people get treatment. As of August 2019, 500 counties in the United States had joined the Stepping Up Initiative's efforts.

CHAPTER TEN

TECH TOOLS

Today, many activists are hard at work to improve mental health for all. **Technology** is playing a big part in spreading awareness about mental health issues and connecting people with the support they need.

Amanda Southworth of Los Angeles struggled with mental health issues in middle school and high school. When she was 13 years old, she created an app called AnxietyHelper. This app provides mental health support to people in need. Today, the app has more than 1,000 users.

Since then, Southworth has created more apps. One is called Verena. It's a security app to help keep LGBTQ people safe.

In 2017, Southworth said that good and bad things happen to everyone. "But it's what we do with the things that happen to us that can make all of the difference," she said.

Amanda Southworth speaks in October 2018 at the Pennsylvania Conference for Women in Philadelphia, Pennsylvania.

CHAPTER ELEVEN

TEEN ACTIVISTS AT WORK

Young activists have done a lot to help people in need. Gabby Frost of the United States was 14 when she founded the Buddy Project in 2013. The Buddy Project works to help prevent suicide. It pairs at-risk people with buddies to help them. Since the project started, more than 200,000 people have signed up to be a buddy.

GABBY FROST

The Buddy Project helps people feel less alone when they're dealing with a mental health problem.

26

GOVERNOR KATE BROWN

Teen activists in Oregon worked to create a new state law. It allows students to take days off from school when they're dealing with mental health issues. In June 2019, Governor Kate Brown signed it into law. This is about more than just giving kids a day off when they feel like it. The law is meant to support honesty about mental health issues. This could help spread awareness about mental illness and work against the stigma.

CHAPTER TWELVE

WHAT YOU CAN DO

The choices you make every day can help build a better future for mental health in our world. Your words have power. You can stop using words such as "crazy" or "insane" in hurtful ways. Use kind words that don't contribute to the stigma against mental illness.

You can also look out for friends at school who may be dealing with depression or anxiety. Offer support and understanding. Notice signs of trouble, such as the person losing interest in things they used to like. The Embrace the Awkward campaign online suggests ways to talk to a friend about mental health. You don't have to be an expert to help. Just be a friend!

If someone you know threatens suicide, tell a trusted adult right away. If the problem is immediate, call 911 in the United States.

Talking about mental health can be uncomfortable—but you can do it!

CHAPTER THIRTEEN
THE FUTURE OF MENTAL HEALTH

The mental health crisis won't be solved overnight. But together, activists, health-care workers, and ordinary people are making a difference.

Young activists are building on the work of those who came before them. Technology has become a good way to reach people in need. People experiencing mental health issues can speak with a doctor or crisis center simply by texting or using an app.

Young activists are also breaking down stigmas by bringing mental health issues into the light. Talking about mental illness is a key part of creating a healthier future.

You don't need to invent an app to contribute to the mental health movement. By reaching out to friends, being honest about your feelings, and listening without judgment, you can support mental health in your own community.

GLOSSARY

abuse (uh-BYOOZ) Harmful treatment.

activist (AK-tih-vist) Someone who acts strongly in support of or against an issue.

advocate (AD-vuh-kuht) A person who argues for or supports a cause or policy.

crisis (KRY-suhs) An unstable or difficult situation.

culture (KUHL-chuhr) The beliefs and ways of life of a certain group of people.

disorder (dis-OHR-duhr) A physical or mental condition.

institution (in-stuh-TOO-shuhn) A facility in which people live and receive care.

juvenile (JOO-vuh-nuhl) Not yet grown.

minority (muh-NOHR-uh-tee) A group of people who are different from the larger group in a country or other area in some way, such as race or religion.

stigma (STIG-muh) A set of negative, often unfair beliefs that a society or group of people have about something.

technology (tek-NAH-luh-jee) A method that uses science to solve problems and the tools used to solve those problems.

therapy (THER-uh-pee) A way of dealing with problems that make people's bodies and minds feel better.

traumatic (truh-MAA-tik) Causing someone to be upset in a damaging way, or related to serious physical injury.

INDEX

A
alcohol, 14
anxiety, 6, 28
app, 24, 30
Arheghan, Ose, 16

B
Beers, Clifford Whittingham, 12
Bethlem (Bedlam) Royal Hospital, 9
Brown, Kate, 27
Buddy Project, 26

D
Congress, U.S., 12

D
depression, 6, 16, 28
Dix, Dorothea, 11

E
Europe, 9

F
Finemind, 19
Frost, Gabby, 26

L
LGBTQ people, 18, 24

N
National Institute of Mental Health, 12
National Mental Health Act, 12

P
Pinel, Philippe, 10
post-traumatic stress disorder (PTSD), 14, 18

R
Reppo, Pavel, 19
Rush, Benjamin, 10

S
Southworth, Amanda, 24, 25
Stepping Up Initiative, 23
stigma, 6, 15, 27, 28, 30
suicide, 6, 14, 20, 26, 28

T
Trevor Project, 16
Tuke, William, 10

U
United States, 6, 10, 13, 20, 22, 23, 26, 28

W
World War II, 12, 13

PRIMARY SOURCE LIST

Page 9
Bethlem Royal Hospital, also known as Bedlam. Colored engraving. About 1750. Now held by the Wellcome Collection.

Page 11
Dorothea Lynde Dix. Deguerreotype. About 1850 to 1855. Samuel Broadbent. Now held by the Boston Athenaeum.

Page 17
Ose Arheghan at the 2017 GLSEN Respect Awards. Photograph. October 20, 2017. Rich Polk. California. Now held by Getty Images.

WEBSITES

Due to the changing nature of Internet links, PowerKids Press has developed an online list of websites related to the subject of this book. This site is updated regularly. Please use this link to access the list: www.powerkidslinks.com/SOOF/mentalhealth